ANNIE LEIBOVITZ
PHOTOGRAPHS

ANNIE LEIBOVITZ
PHOTOGRAPHS

A PANTHEON/ROLLING STONE PRESS BOOK
NEW YORK
Rolling Stone

Copyright © 1983 by Rolling Stone Press, a division of Straight Arrow Publishers, Inc.

All rights reserved under International and Pan-American Copyright Conventions. Published in the United States by Pantheon Books, a division of Random House, Inc., New York, and simultaneously in Canada by Random House of Canada Limited, Toronto.

Leibovitz, Annie.
    Photographs
1. Photography, Artistics.   2. Leibovitz, Annie,
    I. Title.
TR654.L445   1983   770′,92′4   83-2385

ISBN 0-394-53208-2

Manufactured in Japan.

First edition.

For my parents,

Marilyn and Sam,

and in memory

of

Bea Feitler.

INTRODUCTION
BY TOM WOLFE

Has it been duly noted that photography has replaced folk-singing as the favorite delusion of young Americans who want to change their lives overnight? You can spot the poor bozos anywhere. In addition to the cameras and meters slung on straps around their necks, they wear turtleneck sweaters, safari jackets, jeans, and running shoes with soles that stick out like the bottoms of gravy boats. They roam city streets, national parks, and shopping malls, searching for images that will take some magazine editor's or gallery owner's breath away. With only two assets to their names—their cameras and their Great Eyes—they are going to get what Freud said every artist wants: fame, money, and beautiful lovers.

Bearing all this in mind, I hesitate to tell the story of Annie Leibovitz. It can only inflame these feverish dreamers even further.

In 1970 she was a twenty-year-old Air Force brat, as they say, daughter of a colonel, and a student at the San Francisco Art Institute. She was three thousand miles from home. She had no contacts in the worlds of art and photography. In fact, she had spent the year before in a kibbutz in Israel. She was still only a girl, albeit almost six feet tall. She looked like Barbra Streisand elongated by Bernard Buffet. She wore clothes left over from one of the less successful fashions of the Sixties, the style known as Sweatshirt (or Oberlin College) Bohemian.

Even so, one day she turned up at *Rolling Stone* in San Francisco and managed to get the magazine's art director, Robert Kingsbury, to look at her portfolio. That—as in every art student's dreams—was all it took. *Rolling Stone*'s editor, Jann Wenner, took her to New York to take pictures for an interview he was doing with John Lennon. Within a month she had a portrait of Lennon on the cover of *Rolling Stone*.

Over the next ten years she worked steadily at *Rolling Stone* and achieved an eminence in the magazine field comparable to that of Richard Avedon in his palmiest days, when he worked with Carmel Snow and Diana Vreeland at *Harper's Bazaar*. In 1973 Annie Leibovitz was given star billing as *Rolling Stone*'s chief photographer. So far as I know, no American magazine had ever featured a photographer so prominently.

Rolling Stone thrived by running against the conventional wisdom of Late Twentieth Century magazine journalism.

It was presumed that modern readers, particularly young readers, would sit still only for short articles, 2500 words maximum, that were concisely written. So *Rolling Stone* ran articles of ten, fifteen, twenty-five thousand words and encouraged writers to do crazy dances in prose out along the tangents. (In 1973, with Annie taking the pictures, I did a 40,000-word piece for *Rolling Stone* on the American astronauts.)

The axiom in publishing was that a magazine could not survive with a format larger than 8½ by 11 inches (due to the cost) nor with stock other than slick paper (for the benefit of color advertising). Magazine photographers had lamented the demise of *Life* in December of 1972 because it meant the end of the large-size slick magazines. This left *Rolling Stone* as the only national magazine with a large format. In 1974 *Rolling Stone* began printing in full color, on higher grade newsprint, and treating its covers as 11-by-14-inch posters. Annie now had a bigger, bolder layout to work with than even the *Life* photographers had enjoyed, and from that point on her *Rolling Stone* covers became among the most talked about pictures in the business.

When I worked with her ten years ago, Annie's approach combined the journalistic and the formal in the pessimistic manner of two of the great photographers of that period, Diane Arbus and Bob Adelman. Since then she has introduced more humor into her work and emphasized strong, simple, all-over design, partly out of a need to fill the big rectangle of the 11-by-14-inch bled-to-the-edge color covers. Throughout, her work has retained its sharp journalistic sense, and this, for my taste, has given it an appeal quite beyond its formal power.

An example is her picture of Dolly Parton, which is one of the most famous magazine pictures of the past decade. Faced with the task of photographing a grossly over-photographed celebrity, Annie avoided the typical solution, which is to present the subject out of character. Dolly Parton liked to play the part of American cheesecake inflated to the trembling prodigiousness of soufflé. Far from puncturing that impression, Annie decided to inflate it to the exploding point by posing her in front of the male soufflé nonpareil of the Seventies, the bodybuilder Arnold Schwarzenegger. The bust-and-crossbones that resulted is the funniest and at the same time most formally elegant magazine portrait since George Lois and Carl Fischer's picture of Sonny Liston wearing a Santa Claus hat, for the December 1963 *Esquire*.

Annie's photograph in 1980 of John Lennon, stark naked, crawling up the fully clothed torso of his wife like a white mouse was published to gasps of astonishment and shock. The picture ran on the cover of *Rolling Stone* a few weeks after Lennon was shot to death in New York. Annie had been the last photographer he had agreed to see. Lennon wanted to be photographed that way. He wanted to demonstrate his abject devotion to his wife, Yoko Ono, who in the photograph appears sublimely unmoved, even gloriously bored,—by it all. He wanted Annie Leibovitz to be the one to show his grovel to the world.

In the ten years since I first met her, Annie has changed from a shy girl to a woman with a personality like a weather front. She prefers to move in with her subjects days before she starts taking pictures. She moves in like a Bermuda high. We happen to live in an era of skinny topless celebrities. When a camera appears, it's all you can do to get them to keep their clothes on their bony X-ray bodies. But some of the poses in these pages can only be accounted for by the Leibovitz influence. I can't imagine what, other than that, induced Lauren Hutton to pose nude in a mudbath…or Calvin Klein to pose like Sabu gone coy…and I don't even want to conjecture about Robert Penn Warren.

Why are so many celebrities willing, even desperate, to take their shirts off for the photographer? Here we see one of those shifts in fashion that will probably make this book a droll document to review twenty years from now, in the twenty-first century. Until about 1960, show business celebrities (and many literary celebrities), like pimps and gangsters, chose to present themselves in public as less inhibited, more exciting, prettier versions of the aristocrat. Clark Gable was famous, or notorious, in the Forties for taking his shirt off in the movie *Boom Town* and revealing that he wore no undershirt. But in person, in public, in his celebrity photographs, he always dressed as if he were about to pop over, with Doug Fairbanks, Clare Boothe, and the rest of the socially innoculated Yanks, to the Duchess of Ratherwell's on Eaton Square. Whatever else it might have looked like, glamour always looked rich.

In these pages we see glamour succumbing to that great passion of the Sixties, *nostalgie de la boue,* nostalgia for the mud. Quite aside from the way they changed music itself, Elvis Presley and the Beatles removed the tuxedos, foxtrots, and Mid-Atlantic accents from show business stardom. They talked Down Home, they acted Low Rent, and they made it glamorous for stars to look like raw vital proles. But Presley and the Beatles were merely pioneers. The true inheritors and emperors of the mud were the Rolling Stones. One of Annie Leibovitz's most successful portraits is of the Rolling Stones after a 2½-hour concert in Los Angeles in 1975. In that picture you have it all...After the Mud Wallow...Late Twentieth Century glamour in a glowing porcine coat of sweat.

A lovely irony of the mud is that the star as Raw Vital Prole today makes more money than the star as Rich-looking Aristocrat ever dreamed of. Sylvester Stallone, who appears herein nude from the ilial crest up, using his son as a 45-pound barbell, probably made more money from two movies, *Rocky* and *Rocky II,* than Gable did in his entire career as Hollywood's reigning male star. The mud babies make so much money, they can retire in their thirties, like Steve McQueen or Bob Dylan, and become raw vital prole recluses. My favorite picture in this book is of Dylan at the age of thirty-six in 1977, already a recluse, with a thumbnail longer and thicker than Howard Hughes's in his last days and the shriveled red pimento lips of an up-hollow World War I veteran who loves liquor and hates dentists, clamping a Junior Birdman's salute over his eyes for Annie Leibovitz's camera because he has misplaced his dark glasses.

It is in moments like this that Annie Leibovitz transcends the business at hand—namely, the celebrity photograph—and gives us a stiff whiff of the whole gorgeously nutty era of Golden Funk. Dylan, Mick Jagger, Bruce Springsteen, Bette Midler, Woody Allen, they're all here. But I don't think any of the brilliant bawling mud babies in this gallery will impress the reader half as much as the antic eye of their portraitist.

MERYL STREEP
NEW YORK CITY
1981

AMANDA PLUMMER
NEW YORK CITY
1982

RICKIE LEE JONES
LOS ANGELES
1979

DEBRA WINGER
WHITE SANDS, NEW MEXICO
1982

LINDA RONSTADT
MALIBU, CALIFORNIA
1976

PAT BENATAR
ST. PETERSBURG, FLORIDA
1981

CHRISTO
NEW YORK CITY
1981

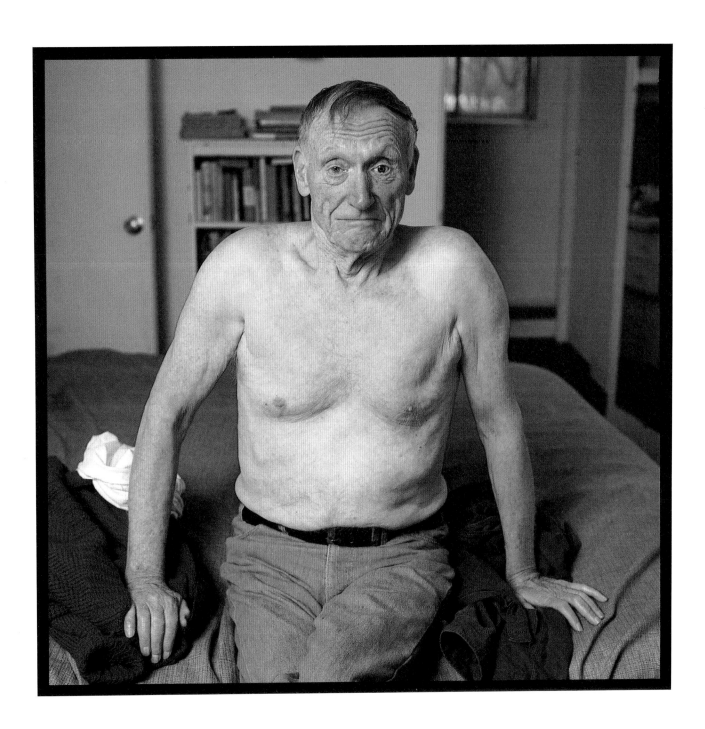

NORMAN MAILER
BROOKLYN, NEW YORK
1982

LIBERACE & SCOTT THORSON
LAS VEGAS
1981

THE ROLLING STONES
LOS ANGELES
1975

KAREN AKERS
NEW YORK CITY
1981

WOODY ALLEN
NEW YORK CITY
1981

JOHN TRAVOLTA
LOS ANGELES
1980

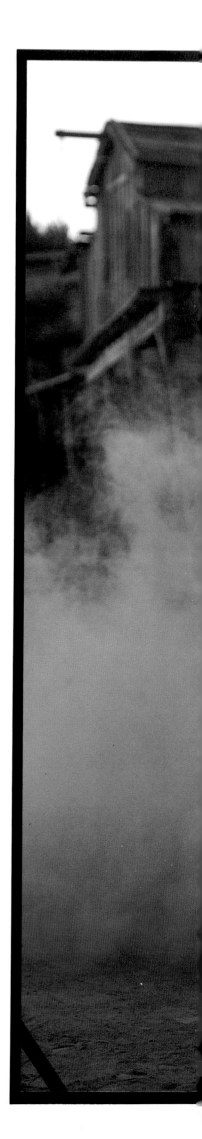

CLINT EASTWOOD
BURBANK, CALIFORNIA
1980

LAUREN HUTTON
OXFORD, MISSISSIPPI
1981

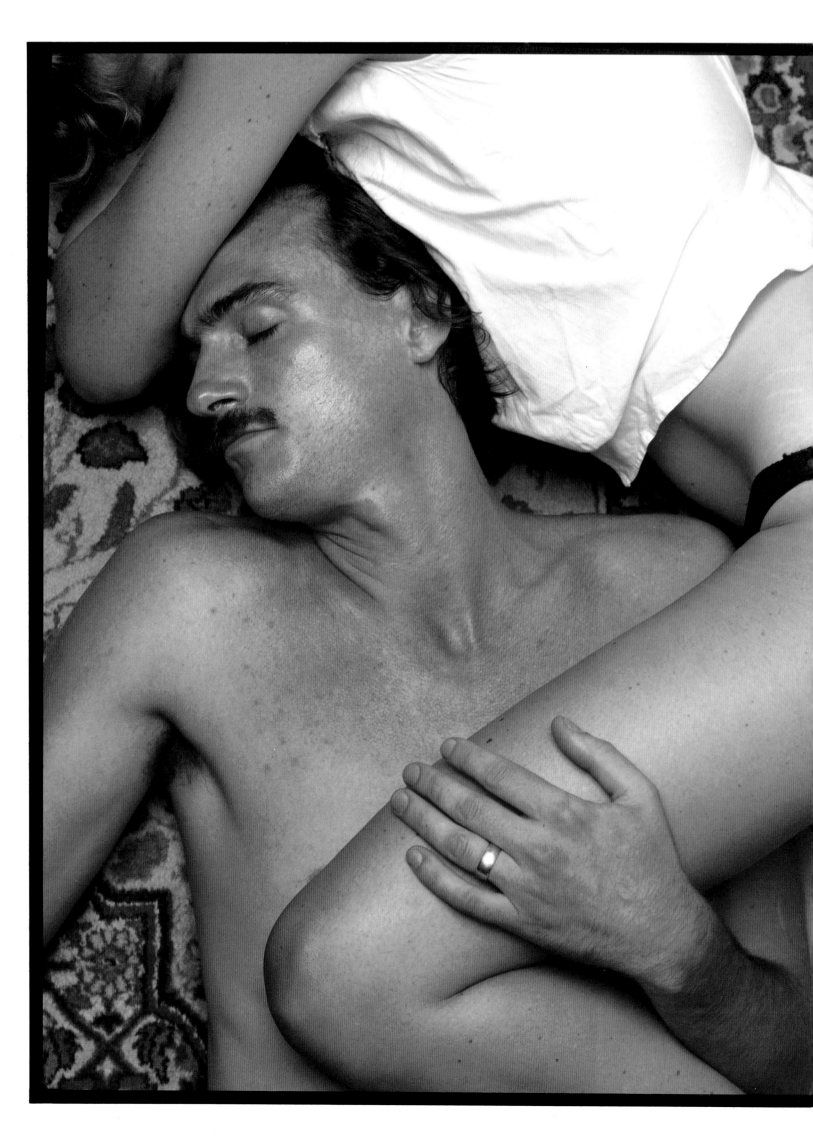

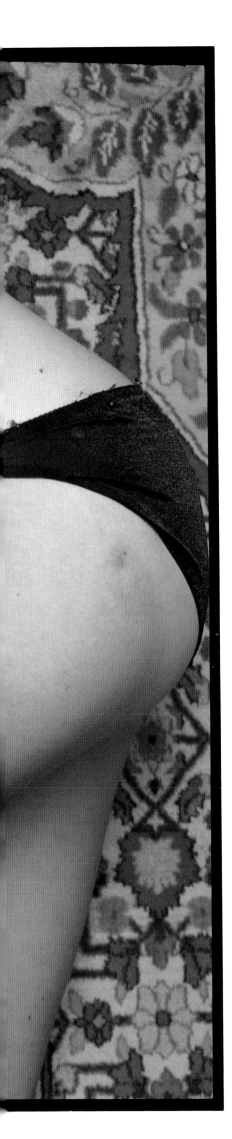

JAMES TAYLOR
MARTHA'S VINEYARD, MASSACHUSETTS
1979

JAMES TAYLOR & CARLY SIMON
MARTHA'S VINEYARD, MASSACHUSETTS
1979

MARIEL HEMINGWAY
KETCHUM, IDAHO
1982

MICK JAGGER
NEW YORK CITY
1980

DOLLY PARTON & ARNOLD SCHWARZENEGGER
NEW YORK CITY
1977

LAURIE ANDERSON
NEW YORK CITY
1982

BOB DYLAN
LOS ANGELES
1977

KEITH RICHARDS
TORONTO
1977

MUHAMMAD ALI
CHICAGO
1978

PALOMA PICASSO
PARIS
1982

BETTE MIDLER
NEW YORK CITY
1979

JOHNNY CARSON
LOS ANGELES
1978

BILLY CARTER & MARGAUX HEMINGWAY
PLAINS, GEORGIA
1977

RODNEY DANGERFIELD
NEW YORK CITY
1980

JERRY LEWIS
LAS VEGAS
1982

WILLIAM HURT
NEW YORK CITY
1981

JERZY KOSINSKI
NEW YORK CITY
1982

JOHN IRVING
NEW YORK CITY
1982

TOM WOLFE
NEW YORK CITY
1980

JOHN BELUSHI
STATEN ISLAND, NEW YORK
1981

MICK JAGGER, RON WOOD,
KEITH RICHARDS, BILL WYMAN & CHARLIE WATTS
NEW YORK CITY
1980

BRUCE SPRINGSTEEN
UNIONDALE, NEW YORK
1981

THE WHO
MINNEAPOLIS, MINNESOTA
1982

PETE TOWNSHEND
SAN FRANCISCO
1980

DEAD HEADS
ASBURY PARK, NEW JERSEY
1980

BLONDIE
NEW YORK CITY
1979

ELVIS COSTELLO
AUSTIN, TEXAS
1982

MICHAEL, DIANDRA & CAMERON DOUGLAS
SANTA BARBARA, CALIFORNIA
1979

TAMMY GRIMES & AMANDA PLUMMER
NEW YORK CITY
1982

SISSY SPACEK
CHARLOTTESVILLE, VIRGINIA
1982

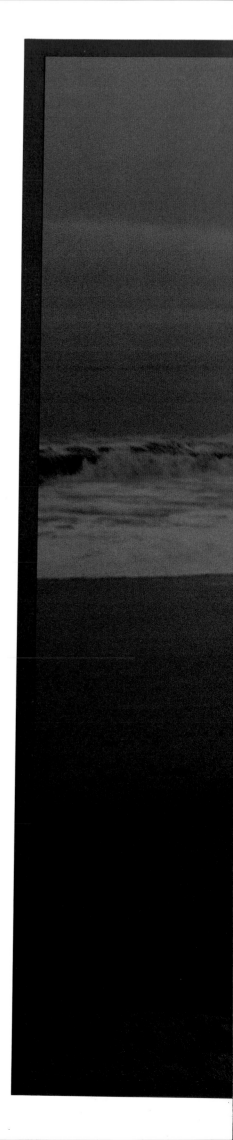

TIMOTHY HUTTON
MALIBU, CALIFORNIA
1981

MATT DILLON
TULSA, OKLAHOMA
1982

ROBERT REDFORD
MALIBU, CALIFORNIA
1980

O.J. SIMPSON
BUFFALO, NEW YORK
1977

BARBARA COOK
NEW YORK CITY
1981

STEVE MARTIN
BEVERLY HILLS, CALIFORNIA
1981

RICHARD PRYOR & LILY TOMLIN
LOS ANGELES
1974

THE BLUES BROTHERS
HOLLYWOOD, CALIFORNIA
1979

PETER TOSH
NEW YORK CITY
1982

JOHN LENNON & YOKO ONO
NEW YORK CITY
1980

YOKO ONO
NEW YORK CITY
1981

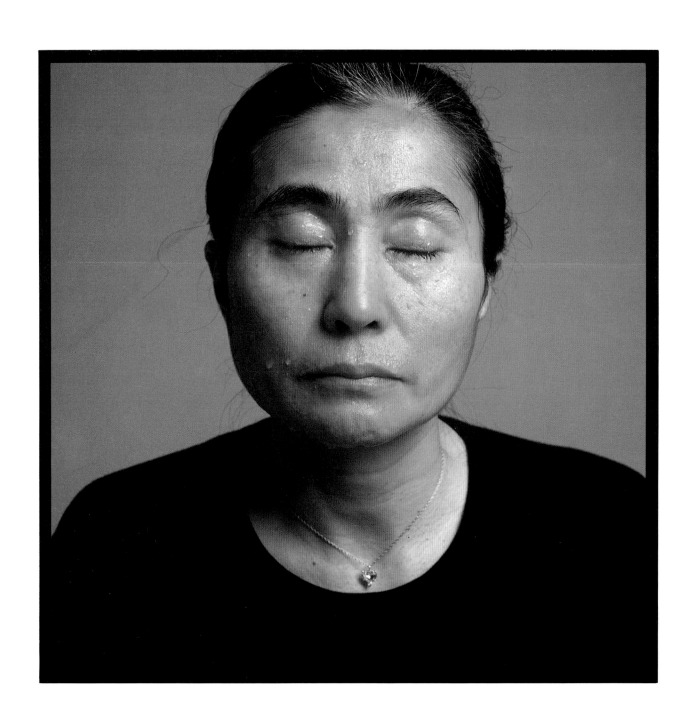

ANNIE LEIBOVITZ

For good reason, based on the vast pulp bulk of evidence, we are tempted to see journalism as an unfriendly art, a sneaky, hit-and-run business out to mock the weaknesses and corruptions of being human. Then, fortunately, someone like Annie Leibovitz comes along and reminds us that journalism at its best is remarkably like friendship at its best, a mutual encounter of open hearts and minds unsullied by prejudice or sentimentality.

I first met Annie thirteen years ago while I was working as a feature editor at Rolling Stone. *I was immediately bowled over by her humor, curiosity, and compassion, these powerful journalistic tools that just seemed part of her personality. She and a writer would go out on a story, and invariably she would come back with more articulate observations than the writer was able to gather. And this was before we looked at her photographs!*

I was amazed at the amount of thought and planning she put into her work. I remember one all-day brainstorm meeting I had with her, Richard Pryor and Lily Tomlin, going over lists of cover ideas and throwing them back and forth; she wanted to be sure that the picture of them to be taken that night would tell the proper story.

The following interview (which is really a conversation between two old friends; if it sounds businesslike, it's because we did it for money) is condensed from two sessions I spent with Annie in her New York studio, in November 1982 and February 1983. In it there's some technical stuff, about color and camera size, and some biographical facts, but basically the interview is about journalism.

For while this is a book of celebrities, clearly Annie all along has been shooting her friends. While it is a collection of portraits, each one tells a story. And while these portraits are from her recent past, they are merely one part of a consistent and continually evolving body of thought and observation.

After the interview I came across this quote of Annie's: "When I say I want to photograph someone, what it really means is that I'd like to know them. Anyone I know I photograph." She wrote that in 1973, in her book Shooting Stars. —David Felton

---

If you were assigned to shoot a portrait of yourself, how would you go about doing it?

Well, you should probably ask me that in about a year, because I'm just beginning to find out about myself. It's funny, for someone who takes pictures the way I take pictures—I have absolutely no idea what I look like. So I'd have to figure myself out, which is what I do, you know, when I take someone else's picture. I try to come to some conclusion about them.

How does that process work? Would you start by doing some research on yourself?

My pictures are really based on the encounter that I have with a person. I'm sure what I do know about them before I meet them is thrown in, but it's really based on the timing and the moment.

The moment and the personal interaction.

The personal interaction and what you ate for breakfast and blah blah blah. That's why it's really such a gambling game. I'm finding more and more that I'm really not in control. It is a collaboration.

Well, let's take someone like Robert Penn Warren, where you weren't that familiar with him before you got the assignment.

I think that picture is based on his humanity. I did read his last book of poetry before I met him, and it was all about time and coming toward the end of life. And I really felt that he had totally accepted life. I had to go back to him three times to accept that he accepted life. "You want to take my shirt off? Take my shirt off." He had a peace about himself in the world. He told me something that only one other person has told me. I asked him what he was thinking, and he said he was thinking about nothing. Lennon told me the same thing, which meant that he wanted to be completely open for what was going to enter him. Robert Penn Warren is so assured of himself that it doesn't matter how he's photographed. I love that.

John Lennon played an important role early on in your portrait work.

He was my first cover for *Rolling Stone*. And at the time—I was still in school at the San Francisco Art Institute—I felt the cover shot was like, you know, the mediocre picture, the secondary consideration. A photograph to me was not a portrait—anyone can do that. I was addicted to hardcore journalism, newspaper stuff, "capture the moment in time," Cartier-Bresson. I liked to combine the composition with action. I carried a camera every second, and I was constantly framing life into little thirty-five-millimeter squares.

So when I shot Lennon I was carrying three thirty-five-millimeter cameras, and on one of them I kept a 105 lens which I used for light meter readings. It was a long lens, I came in close on Lennon's face, and while I was taking the light meter reading, he looked at me and I just snapped one picture. And then I did all my other pictures. But I got back to *Rolling Stone*, and Jann Wenner, the editor, went through the contact sheets and immediately pulled out that picture for a cover. I said, "Oh Jann, ughhhh!" I couldn't understand why he liked that picture. I think it took me these last ten, twelve years to come to an understanding of what that picture was. Maybe I was a little bit reluctant to have somebody look back at me. It was the first encounter.

And that shooting, at the very beginning of my career, set a precedent for my work with anyone of any notoriety or fame after that. Lennon was honest and straightforward and cooperative; he made me feel human right away. I wish there was a more elegant way to talk about this, because it really meant so much to me at the time to be treated well by someone who was so famous, who stood out as a legend in my mind. He made me realize we were all people and we were all here on earth, and it was the basis of how I was to approach everyone from then on.

When you were in art school, did you know you would become a photojournalist, or a portrait journalist, or whatever it is you have become?

No, I thought that I was going to photograph my life. It was going to be my family and my friends. I was heavily influenced by Cartier-Bresson to begin with. I liked his framing. And he would just walk the street and photograph whatever he saw. I loved the idea that you could travel through his eye. But what brought things closer to home was Lartigue's work, when he was photographing his family and his life and friends. And one of the heaviest influences, besides Lartigue, would have to be my own family pictures. I come from a large family, six kids; my father was in the Air Force, and we traveled throughout the United States. The family was always reinforced by pictures. When we looked at the family album it would be, "Oh, that was in Alaska. Here we were in Colorado. Here we were in Texas." And that personal closeness I certainly have incorporated in this portrait work today.

I think I pushed myself into journalism because that's what I thought a photographer did when I joined *Rolling Stone*. That's what I had to be at the beginning of my career. I still think I'm a good photojournalist, it's just that sometimes if you have your eye behind the camera all the time, you miss the most important picture. The portrait work now is really important—I don't know who for, that's the biggest problem I'm having. In the long run I keep thinking this stuff is just chemistry and it dissolves, unless you put it in a special vault or something.

Well, that's a big jump, from getting a job at Rolling Stone *to seeking immortality. Maybe we should back up. How did your interest in portrait work evolve?*

I started to realize that the cover of the magazine was this blank space, this canvas, that had problems of its own, and I really started to enjoy shooting the cover.

When was this?

I think when *Rolling Stone* went to color. I had to change to color, too, and it was very scary. I was glad I came from a school of black and white because I learned to look at things in tones, highlights. Maybe this portrait work was a way of beginning to study color. I'm really glad this whole book is in color because it really defines a struggle I have with color.

Remember, too, that *Rolling Stone* was printed on newsprint, rag print, and ink sinks into the magazine. So the only thing that would make it on the cover were pictures that had two or three colors, primary colors, a very posterlike effect. In a strange way, you almost had to make the color look like black and white. So I developed a very graphic use of form and color just to survive the printing process.

And then about the time *Rolling Stone* moved to New York, we went to a larger format cover—more square—and I changed to a Hasselblad because the size of the camera exactly fit.

Did the process of solving these technical problems for Rolling Stone *affect the content of what you were shooting?*

I found that it was more powerful to use one picture with a lot more information than doing a bunch of small pictures—I was using less space to say more about someone. It's a more formal approach to a person. In other words, instead of spending three days with someone, snapping a lot of snaps that seem to dissipate you, I really try to accumulate it all into one picture.

This book is not a retrospective, it's your most recent work, your portrait stuff. Yet in looking at these pictures, don't you see influences from your whole career?

Yeah. Bea Feitler, the designer I worked with for seven or eight years, always told me that to learn, you have to look at your old work. Bea was the most important person in my work at the time I started this book, and what she said was true. When I looked at the photographs together, I suddenly realized what it was I was doing, what all my work over the last twelve years had evolved to, the style. For the first time I had an identity about my work.

Basically this book is an accumulation of what I've learned, based on journalism. It's a very simple fact—most portrait photographers today come from a background of fashion, and I'm one of the few photographers of my generation who come from a background of journalism. And that is the biggest difference, in a nutshell. That is the difference between my work and your Scavullo or your Avedon or your anyone else. I've had a good, solid background in journalism, and I've gone into this portrait work and I've applied it, and it's as simple as that. I don't think there's any hocus-pocus.

Which means you still feel a picture should tell a story.

Well, what I've heard from some people is that when you look at these pictures, it looks like there's some thought behind them. I like to have feelings about people. In the long run, when I have absolutely no ideas, I really trust my feelings. I was just thinking about Lauren Hutton.

She's a very difficult person to photograph because she's a model and yet she's very down to earth. And she really had a fierce desire to take the picture as much as the photographer. It was like working with another photographer, almost like I was competing with her in inventiveness and creativeness. So I suggest something to her that's a very difficult thing to do. It's a chilly morning and it's mud. I thought it was very symbolic. The ultimate way to photograph a beautiful woman would be to photograph her naked, but because she's a model, she's used as a clothes rack. And the idea of photographing her wearing the earth appealed to her and to me. Also, I've studied anatomy, and in Greek sculpture there's always cloth with the body to show movement.

I had to make a decision whether her face should be in the mud or not. I thought it would be too cosmetic to leave her face out of the mud, but then it was such a beautiful face that at the time I just couldn't see putting mud on it.

Where did this take place?

Somewhere in the South, I forget exactly, on her family's land. She used to fish there and do things with her grandfather. See, that's something I do, too. I like to work with these people where they're going to have the time, and they're going to be bored shitless and have nothing else to do. You know, get them when they're vulnerable.

Anyway, a lot of these things are just instinctive, you know? I don't even think about them. I always considered myself to have sort of an average, middle-of-the-road kind of perception. I don't try to over-intellectualize my concepts of people. In fact, the ideas I have, if you talk about them, they seem extremely corny and it's only in their execution that people can enjoy them. Like the idea of painting the Blues Brothers blue is too stupid. It's just too stupid. But it's something I've learned to trust: The stupider the idea is, the better it looks. Painting the Blues Brothers blue is as stupid as the Blues Brothers being the Blues Brothers. They were taking themselves so seriously about being musicians, they were forgetting that they were actors and comedians. I mean, Belushi was saying, "Did you hear Aykroyd on the harp? Better than Paul Butterfield!" And I said, "*Whoa*...time to remember who you are." That's when my job gets a little dangerous. Belushi didn't talk to me for six months. But Aykroyd always knew it was good. I knew it was good, too. It was a healthy thing to do, it was funny.

Let's talk about some other people you've conceived.

What about Meryl Streep?

Well, I'd worked with her two times previously, I was doing all that fashion stuff for *Vogue*, and one of her shootings was a fashion shooting. By the end of it she was saying, "All I wanted was to be on the cover of *Vogue*, if I'd known it was going to be like this..." They were giving me all these dresses to put on her; as many dresses as I could get on her, they wanted to run. That's when I realized what fashion was—selling clothes.

Anyway, I was scheduled to shoot her for the cover of *Rolling Stone*, *The French Lieutenant's Woman* was coming out, and that week Scavullo had shot her for the cover of *Time*, I think. And she'd had such a miserable time at that shooting—she was becoming this very big star, they wanted her to look like a big star, and she couldn't deal with it—that she cancelled my shooting. So I called up her agent and screamed for forty-five minutes, and finally the agent said, "She won't go anywhere with you. She'll come to your studio and give you between nine-thirty and twelve in the morning, and that's it."

I was shooting Belushi at the time, I had all these clown books around the studio and I was even thinking of a whiteface for Belushi. Actually, I bought the clown books originally for James Taylor who had hepatitis and didn't want to be on the cover of *Rolling Stone* because his face was all yellow.

So she came to the studio and she told me about the *Time* shooting, and she said how she didn't want to be anybody, she was nobody, all she was was an actress. So I said, "Well, be no one, be a mime. Let's try the whiteface." And she really loved it. That's when she started to pull her cheeks out like this—she did that herself. It's just great when that stuff starts to happen.

Some of your pictures, on the other hand, seem very intellectually conceived. The Steve Martin is like a joke.

A joke? This is serious work. Steve Martin, actually, he says to me, "Annie, I've pushed myself in my movies and in my career; everything's gone further except for the photographs of myself." And he was really interested in trying to take a new picture. He had just bought that Franz Kline, it was the kind of thing only museums can afford, and it seemed so strange to have it in his home. And he was just in love with it. He said, "I see myself in that picture."

When I went out there I wanted to do him in tails, but then I realized he was already beyond the tails. This was a way of throwing away the tails so he could move forward—he could have been stuck in that *Pennies from Heaven* genre for some time. Originally we were going to paint him black, put him in the painting, but then I came up with the idea of painting the tux like the painting.

Some shots, like Patti Smith, are highly styled, with a lot of planning.

That's really a good story on how a lot of planning can be worthless sometimes. I had an assistant come out from California—I was just starting to work with assistants then—and I said to him, "Listen, I want this huge wall of flame behind Patti Smith, I don't care how you do it." He said, "I have it all figured out." His idea was like this kerosene-soaked net behind her. Needless to say, it lasted about five seconds, because as soon as it burned out it fell down to the floor. So then we lit big barrels of kerosene and practically burned down the place. I think Patti did get a burn on the back of her *tutu.* The whole backside of her was red.

It's really a lot of fun taking pictures with me. And then I slap them in the mud! And then I hang them from the ceiling! And they say, "I heard you were hard, Leibovitz. I heard it wasn't easy."

Yes, how do you get these people to do these things? You're famous for it! I mean, you got Cartier-Bresson himself to pose for you, and he never allows anyone to shoot him.

Well, that's an old story. I was living in Europe—this was after the Rolling Stones tour, 1975, '76—and Jann called me and asked me to do a photo supplement for *Rolling Stone,* a study of six or seven famous photographers. I figured it was an opportunity to meet anyone who was still alive, whose work I admired, and get paid for it.

Cartier-Bresson was not answering any phones, so I decided to go to Paris and seek him out through his agency, Magnum. I arrived at Magnum, and it was just my luck—Cartier-Bresson walked in. I introduced myself, and he said, well, he didn't pose for pictures, but if I wanted to walk with him to where he was going next, I could. I guess I was this young photographer from the United States and he was trying to be very fatherly. I was very scared because I had to interview him as well as shoot him, so I turned on my tape recorder and started asking him questions as we walked.

We walked across the Pont Neuf Bridge, where he took the famous picture of Pont Neuf Park. I knew his pictures by heart; it was this great opportunity to walk with this great photographer. But I guess I was asking him too many questions, because after a while he says, "Is that tape recorder on?" And I said, "Well, uh…"— I was really flustered—"yes, it is. I am not a writer and I really need to hear you." He got very, very mad, then he said, "Okay, come on." He took me to his home, and I had a wonderful lunch with him and his wife. And he refused to pose for any pictures at all. I asked if I could see him again, and he said, well, he might or might not be going to Magnum tomorrow, in the morning sometime—"Why don't you just stop by Magnum?"

All the way back to my hotel I kept thinking, this is really strange. Here's a guy who's supposed to be a street photographer, why won't he let his picture be taken? So I got up at six in the morning and went over to Pont Neuf Bridge. I was hoping he was going to walk across that bridge, and I thought, well, if he could take pictures on the streets, so could I.

Finally I saw him coming across the bridge, I was nervous as all hell, and as he came by, I stood up and started to shoot him. At first he looked behind him, because he thought I was taking a picture of something behind him. Then he suddenly realized, and he got very mad. He said, "You, you…and I even took you home yesterday, I can't believe…" I didn't know *what* he was going to do—he was really furious. Then he calmed himself down, and he said, "Well, if you're going to take my picture, take a good one." And he posed for a picture.

He let me walk with him to Magnum, and on the way he explained to me that he didn't like to have his picture taken because he wanted to be able to roam the streets freely and shoot freely without someone knowing who he was. If he had his picture published, he would be recognized, and people would freeze up. It made sense to me—at least he explained himself—so I ended up running a picture of him pulling a hat over his face.

Well, what about that—do you think about what effect your picture's going to have on the life of the person you've shot when it's published?

It *is* a responsibility. Some things don't have to be photographed. I solve that problem, more or less, by thinking that if the person I photograph can live with it and likes it…it's important that they are able to live with it as much as I can. But I don't like shocking pictures; I like them to be beautiful more than shocking.

To a certain extent I regret the John Irving picture, and the Jerzy Kosinski, because of the mayhem that was made out them. You know, Calvin Trillin wrote a whole page in *The Nation,* and he went on the David Letterman show and talked for twenty minutes about how ridiculous these guys were to pose as they did. But I had no desire to hurt any of those people—it was just sort of fun. I'm really tired of being misconstrued about that.

And *they* didn't complain. John Irving approved the picture, we got a model release from him. And Jerzy saw the picture. With the Hasselblad I'm also shooting Polaroids now, so people can see the picture right there. And when Jerzy Kosinski saw the Polaroid of himself without the shirt, he was like, "Oh my God, it's so beautiful!" I mean, I don't think people do anything they don't want to do.

In the beginning of my work, I think it was considered more journalistic or something if it was more shocking. But I find that if I let people be themselves, it's even more shocking in a way. In fact, that's really what I'm interested in right now, is trying to take a real straight picture. That's why it was important to include this selection of five black and whites of the Rolling Stones. I felt they should be shot straightforward—classic portraiture. Because they're weird. They're weird, but to me they're classic. In the long run, all you want to see is the person; you can't forget that's what you're really doing, shooting the person. And the more I do this work, the more I just want to be very straightforward with it.

But then how will that separate you from the glamour photographers?

It's not going to. It's going to make me into a big putz. Well, that's what's fun about life, David. It just changes all the time. I mean, today I think the hardest thing to shoot is the face, when I thought just the opposite when I started.

Well, it should be an interesting challenge when you go to do your own portrait. I'd like to get back to that question. In a sense, don't you think you have photographed yourself in this book?

I think so. I derive these things from myself.

I was thinking of the last John and Yoko picture, and your personal input into it.

Their album was coming out, and I really felt that what was so phenomenal about their time together was that they were still together. That was the story to me. And they recognized it, too, because they called their first new single "Starting Over." And I knew I wanted them together in the picture. Then when I saw their album, *Double Fantasy,* and they were kissing, I almost started to cry because I thought, God, that was so beautiful. But it was also a problem because it was sort of what I was planning to do.

I thought maybe it should be an updated *Two Virgins,* something from the past. And I thought of the embrace, them lying naked together, and the embrace is based on something from my life, the way I used to sleep with someone, a very relaxed position. So I had sketches made of them lying exactly like that and I tried it on them. Maybe I learned this from Lennon, but I'm not afraid to take moments from my own life and apply them to someone else's. Which is why I've slowed down myself in my work—I really have to have more of a life. You can't take pictures all the time, you need something to draw from. You start to cheat yourself and you cheat the pictures when you're not living.

Weren't you originally planning to work with Bea Feitler on this book?

Yes. Bea had been dying of cancer for over three years, but it seemed like there was time. She had gone back to her home in Rio, and last spring I talked to her on the phone and she said, "Yes, I'll do the book, but just give me a week's more rest and then come down." So I had my airplane ticket and everything, and I got a call, three or four days later, that she was slipping very fast and not to come. And she died within that week. April eighth.

I put the book aside, I didn't think about it for a while. No one knows this, but at the time Bea died, I just thought I had to continue working...but then I had no reason to work. Because she really would make the most mundane things seem as if they were very special and very exciting to do. She would whip me up.

Then I started to think about things in general, about picking up and trying to work by myself, and I knew the book had to come out. It's basically her book, it's basically most of the work I did with her in the last five years. And I feel that doing this book is like releasing myself, going on to something else, and also releasing Bea from working with me.

I wish I could describe in better detail what it's given me, to have edited this book. I wish I could describe what it has given me from the time she died to now that it's actually being published, to have looked at this work and really studied it and to realize what I have to do from here. I see what I was starting to do in those pictures. I can see how I thought, you know? And it only makes me want to think more before I take a picture, and have a concept more, or understand when to let go of the concept and not have one.

The other day I walked in and saw David Hockney, and I looked at him and was surprised that no one had ever shot him the way that I suddenly saw him. I think it would be very difficult to photograph what I saw, but I saw this old man dressed like a little boy, this older man caught in this idea of a little boy. And I thought that first thought is the picture I'd like to take.

There's just so much to keep learning. You think you know something, and you realize you haven't really been looking that close yet. The face is just a whole other territory. I realized in this collection of pictures that most of them are far away. All these people, they're more my *idea* of who they are than who they are. I just shot Debra Winger again, and I can't shoot her face—I don't know what the problem is. She said to me, "You're never going to take my picture until you shoot my face." And I said, "You're absolutely right."

There's a lot of truth, you know, in a face. It's like the ultimate picture to take—if there's nothing else in it but the face, and you're telling a story. The face will tell you everything. And sometimes when they don't say anything, that's like saying everything, too.

ABOUT THE
PHOTOGRAPHS

Meryl Streep, New York City, August 1981. 2¼″ color. Cover, *Rolling Stone.*

Amanda Plummer, New York City, November 1982. 2¼″ color. Unpublished.

Rickie Lee Jones, Los Angeles, 1979. 2¼″ color. *Rolling Stone.*

Debra Winger, White Sands, New Mexico, November 1982. 2¼″ color. Unpublished.

Linda Ronstadt, Malibu, California, 1976. 35 mm color. *Rolling Stone.*

Pat Benatar, Saint Petersburg, Florida, September 1981. 2¼″ color. Unpublished.

Christo, New York City, 1981. *Rolling Stone.*

Robert Penn Warren, Fairfield, Connecticut, 1980. 2¼″ color. *Life.*

Norman Mailer, Brooklyn, New York, November 1982. 2¼″ color. *Vanity Fair.*

Liberace and Scott Thorson, Las Vegas, 1981. 2¼″ color. *Rolling Stone.*

The Rolling Stones, Los Angeles, July 1975. 35 mm color. *Rolling Stone.*

Karen Akers, New York City, 1981. 2¼″ color. Unpublished.

Woody Allen, New York City, 1982. 2¼″ color. *Family Weekly.**

John Travolta, Los Angeles, May 1980. 2¼″ color. *Rolling Stone.*

Calvin Klein, New York City, January 1983. 2¼″ color. Unpublished.

Clint Eastwood, Burbank, California, 1980. 2¼″ color. Unpublished.

Lauren Hutton, Oxford, Mississippi, 1981. 2¼″ color. Unpublished.

James Taylor and Carly Simon, Martha's Vineyard, Massachusetts, July 1979. 2¼″ color. *Rolling Stone.*

James Taylor, Martha's Vineyard, Massachusetts, July 1979. 2¼″ color. Cover, *Rolling Stone.*

Mariel Hemingway, Ketchum, Idaho, February 1982. 2¼″ color. *Rolling Stone.*

Mariel Hemingway, Ketchum, Idaho, February 1982. 2¼″ black and white. *Rolling Stone.*

Mick Jagger, New York City, 1980. 2¼″ color. *Rolling Stone.*

Dolly Parton and Arnold Schwarzenegger, New York City, 1977. 35 mm color. *Rolling Stone.**

Laurie Anderson, New York City, November 1982. 2¼″ color. *Vanity Fair.*

Bob Dylan, Los Angeles, 1977. 35 mm color. *Rolling Stone.*

Keith Richards, Toronto, 1977. 35 mm color. *Rolling Stone.*

Muhammad Ali, Chicago, 1978. 35 mm color. *Rolling Stone.*

Paloma Picasso, Paris, 1982. 2¼″ color. *House & Garden.**

Bette Midler, New York City, November 1979. 2¼″ color. *Rolling Stone.**

Johnny Carson, Los Angeles, California, December 1978. 2¼″ color. *Rolling Stone.*

Billy Carter and Margaux Hemingway, Plains, Georgia, 1977. 35 mm color. *New West.*

Rodney Dangerfield, New York City, August 1980. 2¼″ color. Cover, *Rolling Stone.*

Jerry Lewis, Las Vegas, 1982. 2¼″ color. *Rolling Stone.*

William Hurt, New York City, 1981. 2¼″ color. *Life.*

Jerzy Kosinski, New York City, 1982. 2¼″ color. Cover, *New York Times Magazine.*

Sylvester Stallone and Son, Los Angeles, May 1982. 2¼″ color. *Rolling Stone.*

John Irving, New York City, 1982. 2¼″ color. *Vanity Fair* promotional material.

Tom Wolfe, New York City, 1980. 2¼″ color. *Rolling Stone.*

John Belushi, Staten Island, New York, December 1981. 2¼″ color. *Rolling Stone.*

Mick Jagger, New York City, 1980. 2¼″ black and white. *Rolling Stone.*

Ron Wood, New York City, 1980. 2¼″ black and white. *Rolling Stone.*

Keith Richards, New York City, 1980. 2¼″ black and white. *Rolling Stone.*

Bill Wyman, New York City, 1980. 2¼″ black and white. *Rolling Stone.*

Charlie Watts, New York City, 1980. 2¼″ black and white. *Rolling Stone.*

Patti Smith, New Orleans, 1978. 2¼″ color. Cover, *Rolling Stone.*

Bruce Springsteen, Uniondale, New York, January 1981. 2¼″ color. *Rolling Stone.*

The Who, Minneapolis, Minnesota, October 1982. 2¼″ color. Cover, *Rolling Stone.*

Pete Townshend, San Francisco, 1980. 2¼″ color. Cover, *Rolling Stone.*

Pete Townshend, San Francisco, 1980. 2¼″ color. *Rolling Stone.*

Dead Heads, Asbury Park, New Jersey, July 1980. 2¼″ color. *College Papers.**

Blondie, New York City, May 1979. 2¼″ color. Cover, *Rolling Stone.*

Fleetwood Mac, Los Angeles, 1977. 35 mm color. *Rolling Stone.**

Elvis Costello, Austin, Texas, July 1982. 2¼″ color. *Rolling Stone.**

Yoko Ono and Sean Ono Lennon, New York City, 1981. 2¼″ color. *Rolling Stone.*

Jim Carroll and Parents, New York City, 1980. 2¼″ black and white. Album cover, *Catholic Boy* (Atco).

Michael, Diandra and Cameron Douglas, Santa Barbara, California, February 1979. 2¼″ color. *Rolling Stone.**

Tammy Grimes and Amanda Plummer, New York City, 1982. 2¼″ color. Unpublished.

Sissy Spacek, Charlottesville, Virginia, March 1982. 2¼″ color. *Rolling Stone.*

Timothy Hutton, Malibu, California, 1981. 2¼″ color. *Rolling Stone.**

Matt Dillon, Tulsa, Oklahoma, October 1982. 2¼″ color. *Rolling Stone.**

Robert Redford, Malibu, California, August 1980. 2¼″ color. *Rolling Stone.*

O.J. Simpson, Buffalo, New York, 1977. 2¼″ color. *Rolling Stone.*

Barbara Cook, New York City, 1981. 2¼″ color. *Vogue.*

Steve Martin, Beverly Hills, California, December 1981. 2¼″ color. *Rolling Stone.**

Richard Pryor and Lily Tomlin, Los Angeles, 1974. 2¼″ color. *Rolling Stone.**

The Blues Brothers (John Belushi and Dan Aykroyd), Hollywood, California, January 1979. 2¼″ color. Cover, *Rolling Stone.*

Peter Tosh, New York City, 1982. 2¼″ color. *Rolling Stone.*

John Lennon and Yoko Ono, New York City, December 1980. 2¼″ color. *Rolling Stone.**

Yoko Ono, New York City, August 1981. 2¼″ color. *Rolling Stone.*

*The photograph was not published, although it is part of a session from which similar photographs have appeared in print.

ACKNOWLEDGMENTS

Jann Wenner made me do this book.

I'd also like to thank Beth Filler, Tina Summerlin, George Lange, Jimmy Moffat and Sarah Lazin for their evaluation, assistance and general bullying in the project.

And for their friendship and counsel over the years I'd like to thank Robert Kingsbury, Bob Seidemann, Roger Black, Mary Shanahan, Robert Pledge, Eileen Kasossky, Hunter Thompson, Mick Jagger, Lisa Robinson and Lloyd Ziff.

And special thanks to Earl McGrath who told me to "snap my shutter and shut my snapper," to David Felton who said "don't listen to Earl," and to Janie Wenner who once again stepped in at the last moment to pull it all together.

—*Annie Leibovitz*

Designed by Carl Barile and Jane Wenner
Edited by Jane Wenner

This book was printed in four-color process by Dai Nippon Printing Company on 106-pound matte coated U-lite paper. The text was set in Devinne, Devinne Italic and Firmin Didot by EP&A Typographers, Ltd., New York City, New York. The book was bound by Dai Nippon Printing Company, Tokyo, Japan.